FALLING IN PLACE

FALLING IN PLACE

Patrick O'Connell

Turnstone Press

Turnstone Press
607-100 Arthur Street
Winnipeg, Manitoba
Canada R3B 1H3

Turnstone Press gratefully acknowleges the assistance of the Canada Council and the Manitoba Arts Council.

Cover design: Doowah Design

Cover illustration: Jeff Funnell

Text design: Manuela Dias

This book was printed and bound in Canada by Hignell Printing Limited for Turnstone Press.

Canadian Cataloguing in Publication Data

O'Connell, Patrick, 1944–

Falling in place

Poems.
ISBN 0-88801-173-3

I. Title.

PS8579.C65F3 1993 C811'.54 C93-098059-X
PR9199.3.O36F3 1993

for Jim Fisher
who overcame

Thanks to Arthur Adamson, Bruce Eason,
Catherine Hunter and David Scott, who listened.

CONTENTS

Allergic to sunlight I keep it all hidden away in my mind.
And do you suppose I am content here in this Age? This
world I would like to slap with my fist. On the buses then,
the strangers come and go. And in a way, Samuel Beckett
was a very religious man. I keep encountering his
characters in my soul. People reduced to a hat. A pencil
stub. Trying to write their way out of the rain.

THE DISTANCE THAT THE DEAD HAVE GONE

I grasp what I can. The rest
is a great shadow.

Phyllis Webb

This is what it reduces to. The curtain in flames.
No one in the back yard but me and the pink flamingo
speaking my name to the twilight which is not quite
convinced by my trembling hands. This is how it all
works out. A two room house without any mail. The
far-off cry of the highway which is waiting to encircle
me. The morally superior landlord who inserts all
his keys in my door.

How there was something twisted once in me until I secured the art of sitting still. Breathing in the dark to the distant hum of the fridge. To the tiny creak in the hardwood floor. While somewhere far outside myself the world clangs on. Violent flowers grow along the riverbank and ravens knock the lids off the garbage cans.

I could have walked forever in the deep September blue. As leaves like tiny skeletons clattered across the road. When each tree was a signal in the smoky air. And I wondered where I'd be this time next year. Maybe in the same abyss counting backwards. Throwing my shoes against the wall. Throwing the window open. And calling.

The beautiful Eskimos in 1901 before the white man came. Crawling out of an igloo to secure some food. Constantly moving. Dreaming of seals. Chiselling some hole in the ice. A fish to wipe their frozen hands upon. Their spiritual response to the dark. Moving this way. Moving that. Until some sacred hand extinguishes them one by one. This is the kind of pain I am talking about Rose.

Some days I am shamed by the light. By innocence.
By my dereliction. By anything forsaking its own
name and surrendering in the labyrinth. The way
the children in the school yard annihilate me
with their raucous songs about the winter. Their
songs about the dark. And I have forseen the end.
Drunk in Shopper's Drug Mart. Stuttering my brand
of cigarettes.

I take my debris. I roll it into a ball. Flick it
away like a disaster. Toward the stricken dogs in
the painted harbour of the street where the lame men
whistle. When even the moon I hold on the tip of one
finger is gone. Lke watching a crow fly from fence
to fence. Leaving no trace in the darkness. No wing
prints.

Here where I begin to translate all my scrawled notes
into a secret code. Like a suicide note that only an
incontinent ghost would understand. Or me, with the
ice in my hair. My chattering teeth and ribbons.
Sky-diving out of windows into the happy hunting ground.

The howl has its usefulness. The way it will want to
leap right over the bed and gather me in. And because
I was expelled to the coalbin to be some clacking
skeleton with a vision I will know what they mean when
the sound of their sorrow comes. It will be as easy
or as difficult as breathing. I will show them my crazy
feet. Undressing in a grass shack constantly in ruin
as if I were a deer caught in the headlights and the
rosy neon burned.

There must be something I can tell you about this room.
Where I was born again and died again and dried out with
my heart in a sling. The oriental pattern of the rug.
The bug on the floor I decide not to kill. Priding myself
on that. My terrible benevolence.

To stumble upon the stubborn truth. To know what I mean when I say I am aching. This hollowing out. This emptying. Somehow wounded by beauty and the bondage of self. How after years of it my howling rage died and crawled away into the hills. Where I discover myself half frozen. Out on the narrow horizon. Waving a white glove. Saying I want to lie down. On this highway.

Finally I came. I arrived partly broken. There was
nowhere else to turn except to the ecstasy of my
despair. Long past the angel in the graveyard who
called to me. When I began to perceive a leafless
tremor on the wind. Thinking I had been here before.
The screen door which opened onto nothing. Remembering
my own mother then. Her upside-down smile out in the
garden. But there were the northern lights. There
was always something I could turn to.

It was difficult learning to breathe. But it was even more difficult learning to forget. Though in the end I learned both to breathe and forget. Sometimes I juggle one orange while I do this. Breathe and forget. So it is ok to be here where the rose is torn. Where the streets are a jungle of burnt glass and the world has blood in its eye. Breathe and forget. It's what I told the paper-boy. For a christmas tip.

How I was born to this vigilance. This holding on.
This letting go. Where I ring the bell for Pavlov's
dog. Light my arrow on fire and circle the wagon-
train. Then throw my stone into the sky's reflection.
Where these hands of mine teach themselves to pray.
Running naked past the circus tents. Swallowing a
sword. Breathing this purple flame.

I celebrate the birthday of one who departed. Time out
to remember the terrible scheme. Like the total silence
of a room lost in twilight. Where a pin drops leaving
a tiny echo. And now the simple speech of a songbird.
How lyrical the world is in spite of all my loss.
Walking across the room and closing the shutter. To the
sound of rain starting on leaves.

To see your own reflection in an instant in a storefront window. Startled by your own wooden face. Your naked hands like little prayers of their own that knuckle towards the convoluted sky. Confronted by yourself at last. Your own complicity. Tip-toeing along the boulevard hoping for redemption. Only to find an old cigarette paper stuck to your shoe. Sometimes you rise and then you fall. Making your way across bridges. Over the old ghost you might say. Or the mist on the river.

Ridiculous in my fear, my need, I cartwheel into the
dark. Hesitant at first but going deep into the world.
For how was I to know my prayer would be answered and
my God would be like a ricochet off a rock. Like a bird
that descends in the paralysed air into my baptism of
fire. And I would turn. Into the gathering dark.

And so the woman clearing tables in Eaton Place speaks
to me of spring. How some man with forty oil wells and
an airplane is coming to fly her away. Talks about
her divorced husband who followed her to Vermillion Bay.
To Toronto. Wherever she goes. She says he is a stone
around her neck. An albatross. And all she ever wanted
was to fly.

I am looking at a photograph of me when I was sixteen.
Already programmed for the highway. Like the tramp
I saw in Tim Horton's who dropped his bedroll on the
floor like a sack of old shoes. Stirring his coffee
with a pencil. Laughing crazily into his cup. Like
a man who has met the beast. Within.

Through the tangled streets then. Back to a room. Where my only rose is bleeding. Where I hold my picture of Buddha up to the light. Clank the stove upon the kettle and begin. A journey across hardwood floors. Losing a shoe and a cigarette. Thinking there might not be a salvation of any kind. Just snow upon the windowsill. Some useless door. Banging in the wind.

The way George died at 86. In a room full of dusty model ships that he had built to beat the boredom. In April I pry George's window open so he can breathe. I wipe his ass. I iron his shirt. I put his shoes on and I lace them up. I bring him groceries, a meat pie and two bananas, that he pays me for. By the door he makes a nervous joke. I laugh with him. But I do not mention hope.

I guess I have not written for a couple of weeks and
a lot of water has gone under the bridge. Where I
was kneeling once with my own tin drum. Reading about
Grecian Formula and Rocket Richard who banged a yellow
hole in the sun. Hearing hollow voices now as if I
were a radio and you could tune me in. This is your
commander here it is saying. And we are all alone
drinking up the aftershave.

I threw my holster from the bridge into the river. And
surrendered then. The only way I knew. Eyeball to
eyeball with the wreckage. The river full of rusty cans.
The sky like a burnt-out lightbulb. Loss and denial.
The way I figure my own speed. Smoking my way across the
horizon. Getting lighter every day now. Nearly airborne.
Touching the bruise on my skin.

There was the snow and I tracked through the streets. The wreckage of winter. The wreckage of finding myself again where I am. Long past the twilight lost in a splintered window. A bit of snot on my sleeve. Talking to dead men on park benches. Trying to make them remember. That they were here.

No tears. I keep waiting for the tears that must have
dried up like a desert. That's it. The desert. Where
I am naked. Nailed onto a black rock. Spread-eagled.
A nervous scorpion walking across my hairless chest.
You are what you teach they said. And I searching madly
through my dictionary. For the meaning of sand.

FALLING IN PLACE

And even though it all went wrong
I'll stand before the Lord of Song
with nothing on my tongue but hallelujah

Leonard Cohen

PHASES OF THE MOON

Here where I die and I do not die
        I find myself
                        returning
trying to form my own heart
into the shape
                    of a wing
for before I can be found again
I must accept the loss
of a willow that was bending
in my mind
this leap I make
                into the darkness
here where the arrow is
                            I am
learning to breathe
learning to walk out
                        on desire
this is how I come to you
in all my rags and ribbons
as if I were an acrobat
                            in blue
travelling on a wire
silently asking
            for my deliverance

THE MORNING STAR

I suppose it began with the light
    this sitting still
                I mean
as calm at last
as the stones by the river
                that speak
and I
    who was always turning
    or hoping to turn
but never much afraid of air
    or the ragged edge
                of beauty
O how the heart
                gathers itself
    and goes
            past closed doors
    strewing roses
to the sound of wind
            in poplar trees
the sound of hooves
                in the alley

•

It begins with the breath
that after a time
will form itself completely
this is what you must remember
completely
now look
see how the sky
is round
and when you return
you discover the breath
so it begins
you are constantly moving out there
and returning
what echoes then
what you turn to
now that the sky has opened
like a hand

THE MORNING GLORY

Because I can change my mind   I change
      my mind
            and go
past whatever bloomed in me
                        in August
      hollyhocks in a back lane
the scent of the calm Earth
                        after rain
      this celebration
                  of rain
      upon my tongue
this gradual perception
                  of my life
            on the mend
where I have to reckon with
                  what you would call
      the dark
these simple shoes then
                  that walk themselves
                              and I
past the thick and thin
                        of the garden

METAMORPHOSIS

By seven years of age   I could walk
        a railing
        by ten I confessed
        life was hell
        and by twelve
I had already become
                                        a saint
        performing figure-eights
        on one skate
dispensing quarters like communion
        to the homeless
and was last seen
                                by a caribou
        my hands formed in prayer
flying straight
                                    over the tundra

•

Time figures prominently
                            call it negative space
the part you would never touch
                                      with a crayon
and in spite of this truth
the world is what it is
sweeping its yellow leaves
                                  into a bag
where we can begin
                          simply to be
Time we said laughing
                    doing a dance on our grave

THE WISDOM OF TURNING

How could I sing   when I had not slept
      the night before
though somehow I managed
                                        to rise
how mostly I managed to rise
                                          and fall
where I had shaved and whistled
and heard the sound of my bare feet
      go slapping
                        across the floor
here where the night blooms once
and the moon and darkness
                                      sail
to the sweet ticking
                              of my Swiss clock
where everything
even the ladybug on the screen
the scent of rain
                        softly drifting through

LISTENING TO THE HOUSE

for Claudia Scott

I could see myself   diminishing
    in the dark
so I did a somersault
        like every skylark
    in Idaho
for maybe it was the sky
        or the shape of seashells
    that made me stay
some moment of exstasis
            on the spiral stairs
    where I first beheld
                the way
and I xeroxed a signal
                to you
I was listening to the house
knowing at last
            there was an opening
some room where I swept
    with my August broom
and everything turned
                into blue

•

The wind somehow made out of leaves
windsong as lyrical
as any flute
this night where you are
contending
saying ‘be content
and there will be enough’
then lighting a rose
and throwing it onto
the highway
for what starlight there is
falls across the road
it staggers
over the canyon
and yours is the face
you aspired to
you are the one
who let go

WINTER SOLSTICE

Because I do not hope   I do not doubt
      and move easily
            among the citizens
certain of my conviction
      my turning toward
            the rose
this is how I dream these nights
      as if it were carved
            in bone
my inner weather
      the field
            in my mind
having come full circle
on the shortest day
            of the year
inch by inch
      in the falling dark
walking along the railroad track
with the sound of the sea
            in my ear

AWAKE AMONG THE SLEEPERS

Beholding the grace that you find
        to go on
        not knowing how
        into the colour
                        of darkness
while far below you
        the world speeds
        over the edge
then taking care of details
                like any lover would
a man ties up his shoe
puts his face against
                the window pane
        in a white room
        with a curtain
                        blowing in
how there are certain words
you say over and over again
        like sky
                or laughter
thinking somehow the words
                        will save you

•

By the autumn river
shaking the old oak tree
as all the acorns
fall
the way the night
invites me
to this calling
what sings to me
what I reach for
on the inside
the pivot that I turn upon
being my skin

JOY WILL FIND A WAY

As my salt shaker jumps in my sugar bowl
        and my spoon and my fork
                                        do a jig
I belly-dance across my room
        blowing kisses at you
if you want to be beautiful
                              you have to laugh
put a lampshade on your head
        snap your fingers
                              and order flowers in
        from Amsterdam
throw your feathered hat as far as you can
        tell me dreams
                              how laundry soars
        on the lines
like dark lustrous children flying
                                        everywhere

THE SPIRIT OF THE VALLEY NEVER DIES

for Angele Arpin

And so I came to find myself
        alive
                in the circular dark
watching the stars
                        take the town by surprise
how I found my own salvation
                                in the moonless night
and let the past go
                                gradually
as if it were a small bird
thrashing its wings
                                        in my fingers

•

A quill for writing crow tracks
across the moon
the way the heart was then
before its birthing
knashing its own knuckles
on a rock
the way the sky was then
and you trying to find
your way back
a witness to the starry night
who strikes her light
upon a bone

THE MAN WHO BURST INTO LEAVES

The emptiness that rushes to embrace me
    striking it rich
        in my elegant soul
like some private victory
            I could score
    against the darkness
    where I win
        an olive branch
    a moment's ruin
all those choices that I made
            or didn't make
how it came to me
        like God's hand in the world
like some giant step I could take
    into the smoke blue
            air
casting a cold eye on passion
then somehow finding
            'the rage to live'

•

Somehow I knew
                              I belonged
          to the night
I knew these hands
were for loving
the clearing you come to
after all
            the bric-a-brac
the ways of a heart
that somehow knew
                                 the night
       is a bird
and there is a light
                               inside

FALLING IN PLACE

Not knowing if my tongue will be heard
                                        by the darkness
but to gather all fortune together
      and become
      this night I have earned
this pirouette I want
      in the space of an empty room
knowing the fullness
                                      of my longing
      listening to my night voice sing
      O Earth
I move haltingly towards you
to some small place in the grass
                                          where I wait

SCABB IN THE DEEP

There is always my story of course
when all else fails

Samuel Beckett

Scabb limps   says
it is a fact of life
having jumped out the window
on the 7th floor
of the McClaren Hotel
hitting the marquee
on the way down
which broke his fall
so he limps now
wide in the hips
thin wristed
saying what the fuck
is this noise
Kraft Dinner for christmas
and having the nerve
not to say grace

Scabb knows   life burns
and admits it
to his welfare worker
who sighs
who asks him questions
as if to determine
if Scabb is insane
and Scabb plays along
stuttering badly
I-I-I
thinking the bread
might come in handy
thinking of all the deals
he could make
with the vouchers
though at least he never spoke
to those men
in the doorway
who beckoned
he had his own angel
over his shoulder
who whispered to him
that he was alone

Scabb can dance   though
he can only dance
alone
sitting in the Aberdeen Hotel
peering at the bar maid
through the bottom
of his beer glass
dropping his wooden nickel
into the jukebox
O Christ he thinks
a 30 lb muskie on the wall
lunging   for the women's can

Scabb begins   like any Fool
he begins
but finishes nothing
except the picnic lunch
he eats
by the smoky marsh
where all the autumn geese
are gathering
how he loves all those V's
in the sky
all that honking
eating his onion sandwich
in stale bread
saying he was cursed
by the darkness
though he never gave in

Scabb   in the corner
in his rotting jockey shorts
shadow boxing the wall
aware
of his aggravation
when the church bell rings
I don't need a wife
he says
I need a skin magazine

Scabb's pain   festers
when he sees his teapot
in the pawnshop window
for sale
for 5 bucks
and finally
drunk
Scabb passes out
in the back seat
of a cruiser car
completely stunned
by the horn
of a passing freight train

Scabb   hurling his burned out wallet
at the door
coughing into his hands
jerking off in a cracked mirror
with a neon moon
Scabb fucked the mop last night
and there is more
he keeps an old ballet slipper
in his bed

Scabb   on desperation duty
as an empty wine bottle
rolls across the sidewalk
and falls into the gutter
with a clank
Scabb   mesmerized by twilight
by the cold iron sky

While out in the street
a green garbage bag
full of angry wind and tumbling
like some tormented beast
on the run

Scabb   in jukebox twilight
orders more beer
seated with an aboriginal
in the Manwin Hotel
who speaks of timberland
the gathering of wild rice
in a canoe
the way goose eggs
are perfectly round
and when the aboriginal
finally goes for a piss
Scabb scoops all the change
off the table

Scabb   back on the boards again
at Main Street Project
having gobbled some pussy
on Martha Street
weeks ago
drinking cheap sherry
like rain
in his busted cowboy boots
his dinosaur ring
his double-breasted suit
saying to the alcohol counsellor
I want to give my life now
to Jesus

THROWING MY SHOES
AT THE MOON

And if the earthly no longer knows your name
whisper to the silent earth: I'm flowing.
To the flashing water say: I am

Rainer Maria Rilke

Because beauty is always relevant I am trying to sew this eagle on my coat. Trying to let go of the room that somehow smells like joss sticks. The tiny click the fridge makes when it kicks in. Here at the centre of my own departure where the crystal twilight tricks the glass and I begin. Stitch by stitch. For this is the time before the darkness ever was and I forget. How I came to be here. How I closed my eyes to see the light. Like the time on the mountain in Montreal when I saw the Tai Chi dancers. And I knew I would have to learn how to pray.

On the hope side of the circle game I rise above and move across these stubble fields as if they were burning. How I am into my own return now like some salmon trying to swim up a waterfall and I move back to the beginning and the end with every breath I take. Here where I diminish nightly only to be replenished by the sky and moon. How I was there in spite of the holes in my blanket. In spite of the leaf in my shoe. Bowing to you the way the grass bows down to the wind. And this is what it is that moves me through the universe. This knowledge of my skin. Knowing I could be saved by the rain. By my own letting go.

It's good enough. This space I have carved out of the darkness. Having yanked the nails out of every board and built this tiny pyramid where I celebrate and sorrow. As if I were the sea giving away to the moon some nights when there is the cry of a gull. Gulls on the purple horizon. The way there was the summer moonlight in our bed. My hands all tangled up in your hair. Trim boats bobbing on the fishing boat sea. Because we were content, because we were satisfied, everything came to us. Even the light in the morning. The scent of salt in the air. The pure white silk of the sky.

So the river breaks up and I stand on the bridge and see my own shadow on the water. Now I am sure where to turn. Having walked away from edges. Having spent years courting the dead. Sticking my tongue to a wrought-iron fence while holding the string of a kite in the air. And now languish in the cool centre of these rooms. Extinguishing all my candles one by one. As the cat runs across the piano keys inventing a tune of its own. Like any free man I have learned to lie down in the darkness. Knowing there is a river in me somewhere. That is breaking up.

So in the end I turned to emptiness, to silence, because it was the last house on the block. Hustled by beggars and the rush of my skin I think I could get free if I were vigilant. Feeling my life has already changed here in the vibrant air. The broken-saw song of crows touches me with the memory of spring. I have crossed this bridge I think 35 years ago in a pair of old runners. Though I have no sacred legends to tell. Only something pushing up in me that I have to write down. Like the night when the bird flew into the room. Claiming everything.

The way the wind breaks all its bones in the trees. When language fails and all that I know is the nuance which I cannot explain. Now the words are caught in my throat again as if I had no voice of my own. Having surrendered. Having fought the crows back. A midnight talker who knows it all comes and goes sparked by love. Birds so high in the morning sky I can hardly see them. Specks in the distant blue. An old man sleeping on a painted bench. A rusty harmonica in his hand. Lost his heart out on the avenue where he went begging for night.

I tell you it is only death that keeps me sane. Otherwise I would collapse under the weight of my own skin. Where all by themselves my two shoes do a dance in the dark. Voiceless I sing. Sailing through streets littered by yesterday's papers scurrying in the wind. The river full of September leaves. Trying to rule things out and glide slowly into the arms of my keeper. How there was a bobcat in the yard last night. And the cook showed up for work drunk again. On the way to the airport a white dog ran up to lick his hand. A window opened up somewhere. There was a face with a watering can.

This is for all the sorrow that will come down the road. This is for the spaces I haven't been in yet. This is for the fragments of my life that lay collapsed upon the hill. That I gathered together as if they were leaves and placed in a paper bag. It's not that easy to forget. Mostly I remember that I was alone. How in the end I buried myself in the fever. Having veered dangerously close to edges I knew there were things that needed to be said. What I was trying to do sounds so simple. To take my shoes off. And merely climb into the sky.

It's true there was a light around my body then. There was a road and for the moment at least I had been redeemed. Touching the birthmark on my skin. Learning the language of animals. Seeking my fate in a circular field a spiral that I finally reached with my hands. Everywhere there was the sound of the sea. Near the end of my crazy sorrow I watched the sky changing colour before my very eyes. Turning incandescent red in the evening when I sang my chant. Everywhere I reached out for you. Now and forever. World without end. When every shooting star was a bird on fire flying towards a lake.

Coughing up the whole truth again. How I am halfway in and halfway out of the dark. Having made my way through cobbled alleyways that have already forgotten the ring of my heels. And the tiny trail I left behind. The scent of soap. My fingerprints on fenceposts. Spent sunflower seeds all the way into the garden. Here on the worn planks of the garden. To have been here as long as I was asking for the light. What I had always mistaken the darkness for.

Pleased for one instant just to have seen that face in a crowd. Rain splashing silver into the street. Somehow lost in this labyrinth of splendour I find my way. Knowing I would crop up like stones in a field in April. Once in a lifetime the veil gets lifted and I get a glimpse. I say everything comes from God. Even nothing. Knowing I grow more vulnerable day by day. Thinking of the one line that could have saved me that I uttered to myself one time over the grub. How I wait and I do not wait. Having grown so calm now a bird nests under my skin. This is what exists in my memory. The possibility of light. A space between the spaces where I occur.

How there was a face that made me stay. That loomed up out of the darkness like an echo. And I began to yearn. Where there always was the element of fire. The smoke that rose like incense in my mind. And I performed the miracle of bending. How an aging man in a detox learns to bend. Inspired by some photograph of emptiness nailed onto the wall. While somewhere far outside itself the sky finds its own way home. How mostly we win and we lose. How I was left with the words I pulled one by one out of a silk hat. Holding up my cue card. Trying to take my signals from the sky.

Here where I bloom and fade in every given moment as if I were the wind trying to return. The taste of my own ashes on my tongue. How I spent it all in streets that curved like the woodwork of a violin. I played out the song of my life in those cobbled roads where I died in the rain. Risking everything for love. The swagger of my own skin that moved across the universe. Barefoot now with no leather. Making my pitch on Main Street. Redeemed because I am able to let beauty go.

The way my body survives and remembers the light when the white butterfly flew onto the edge of my cup. The way the burst seedpods drift past the window in May. Past the garden. The dove on the telephone line. A memory of a rain soaked lane where I went with the garbage. With my worn out shoes in a bag. How it was a matter of waiting and allowing the silence to happen. As if time could exist without a grievance. The way it returns to me. The fragrance in my yard that spring. The scent of spring fields blowing in from the south. The way I lived on both sides of the tracks. Going back and forth like a bee.

There was always the moon in the morning suspended above the trees. Each day I retraced my own footprints past that image. Everywhere else the world was less coherent. Less content. Somehow lost in its winter snow like the iron traffic that bangs across the bridge. This incredible voyage. How do I end. How do I learn the tricks of the heart that survives. As if I could crack the winter open like a walnut shell. As if I owned a mirror in which nothing was ever reflected. And then some window in which a face appears. Asking me to win.

One thing participates in another. I could be this leaf then that has let go. That has tried to spin its way to earth hoping for some connection. Hoping for some stubble field in which I could begin. Translating the darkness. Trying to put my heart in place as if I were a warrior going up against the chaos in his soul. How I long to lean out of windows in my shirt-sleeves and shout out my redemption. I want to enter into the circle of my own song. As if I were leaves or some field in September that a man is burning tonight.

So I had to ascend and I did and was given a key. Somehow I had to make it work. And maybe that's what it was. A colossal blossoming. Having been homeless on a swing for years haunted by my blood. My fierce desire. How I wanted my life to exist I invented a meaning. I learned to sit still. I learned when to sing and not to sing in graveyards. The way I went down streets like a shaman blessed by the colour white. Armed in the end with silence I wanted to go for it as if there were a rose in my teeth. And I was sky-diving naked. Into the world.

What I came with and how I surrendered in time. Letting the contents of my mind go. Free from my own iron grip then I simply walked away recalling the word I had spoken. The promise I had made. The vow. Everywhere I went I found my own returning. Some fragment of a wing that tracked across the sky. A crow patrolling an alley. And where the dead men were and will be I can say that I have gone breathing deeply. In the end, which was everywhere, I could say that I came. It was spring and it wasn't spring. I had my coat collar high. They were waving to me from the other shore.

Photo: Sandy Brown

Patrick O'Connell is a Winnipeg writer whose first poetry collection, *Hoping for Angels*, is also published by Turnstone Press. His previous occupations include teaching, photography, jewellery-making and work in the mental health field. In 1993, he was nominated for the John Hirsch Award for Most Promising Manitoba Writer.